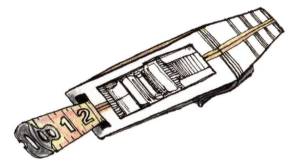

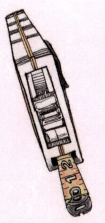
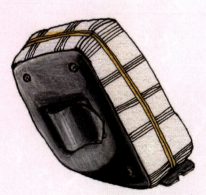

If You Give an

Architect a Contract

WRITTEN BY **Seth Kaufman**

ILLUSTRATED BY **Laura Lee Pedersen**

For Theo and Hilary.
For homeowners everywhere,
including architects and contractors.
— S.K.

For Ilima. — L.L.P.

If You Give an Architect a Contract
Text copyright © 2013 by Seth Kaufman
Illustrations copyright © 2013 by Laura Lee Pedersen
All rights reserved. Published by Sukuma Books
ISBN:9780985626594

First Edition

This is a work of fiction. Names, characters, places and incidents either are the product of the author's imagination or are used fictitiously. Any resemblance to actual persons, living or dead, events, or locales is entirely coincidental.

If you give an architect a contract,

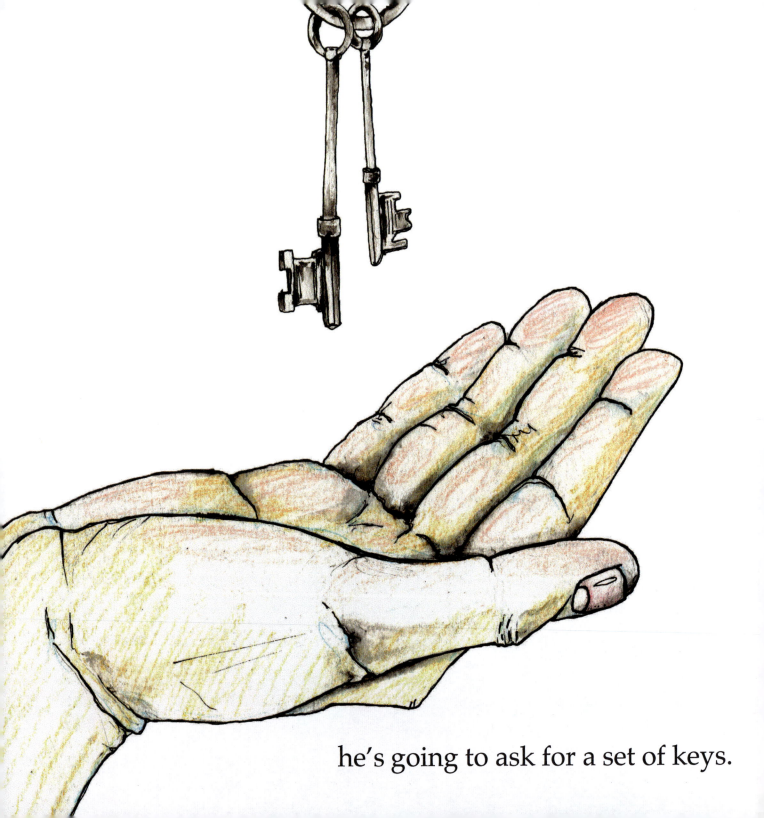
he's going to ask for a set of keys.

When you give him the keys, he'll jiggle them,

which will remind him of money, and he'll probably ask for a deposit.

When he pockets your check,

he'll tell you that the initial plans will be ready in four weeks.

A month later you'll start checking your email, voice mail and snail-mail for the plans,

not realizing your architect is busy finishing three other projects.

By week six, you'll call your architect,

and he'll probably say he's glad you called because he's just finishing your plans and is going to send them tomorrow.

When the plans arrive three weeks later, you'll ask yourself if this is the house you discussed, because some aspects—the kitchen, the bathroom or the deck, or maybe all three—

are exactly what you didn't want.

After eight weeks and two revisions you'll get a plan you can live with.

And that means you are ready for…

Just as you drop three olives into a martini,

the architect will stop by again to discuss the bids, which have materialized with astonishing speed.

He'll push quality over savings.

But when you pick the cheaper contractor, he'll say, "Great choice! I'll meet with him tomorrow."

So you'll give the architect another set of keys,

which will remind him that he has an invoice for you.

And the next morning you'll pay the invoice because, unfortunately, you were raised with good manners.

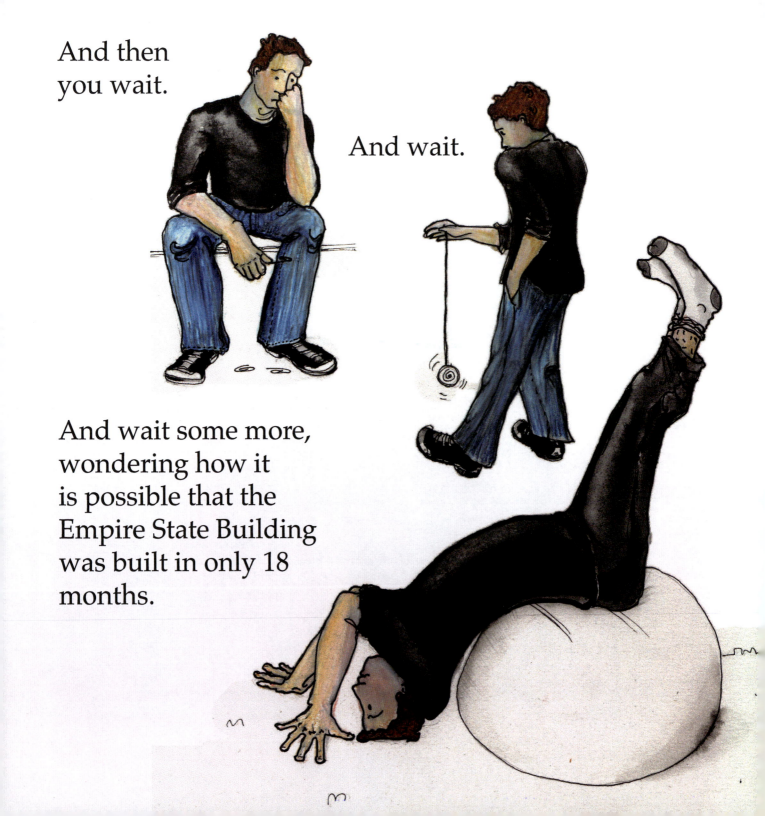

And then you wait.

And wait.

And wait some more, wondering how it is possible that the Empire State Building was built in only 18 months.

When the crew finally shows up four weeks behind schedule,

you'll kick yourself for studying French in high school—as opposed to Spanish, Bengali or Mandarin—

because nobody speaks enough English to tell you where the boss is.

So you get the contractor and the architect on a conference call.

So you'll go to the liquor store for more vermouth.

There you'll bump into a friend who says your contractor has 12 people working at a house on her block.

When you get home, you probably won't open the vermouth.

Instead, you'll fill your martini glass with gin.

Then you'll call the contractor and demand he put six men on the job.

Next day he'll come over with three guys.

After six weeks, you'll ask for an estimated completion date.

Your contractor will say, "Seven weeks, no problem."

But he'll stare at the ground when he says it.

Which means you can't trust him.

So you can't plan a vacation,
or when you'll move in,
or when new furniture should be delivered,
or when to switch the phone.

Nothing.

So you'll tell the contractor that if construction delays continue, you will delay payments.

And so crews of six or more will start showing at your house.

Even on Sundays.

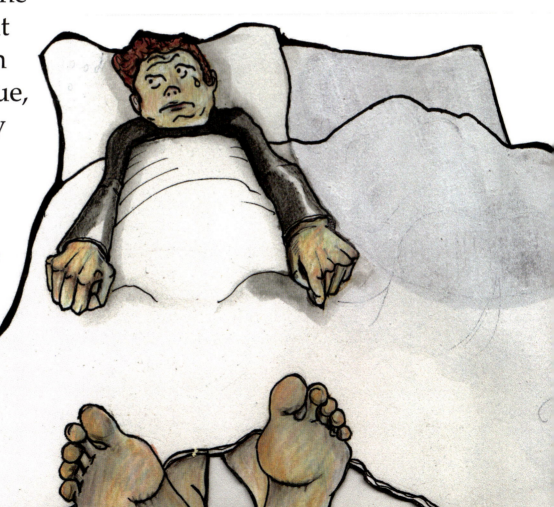

Two months later, when the house is finished, the architect will come by.

He'll probably pull out a camera and tell you how the renovation has increased the value of your home by half a million dollars, which you know isn't true.

So you rush him out the door with a lie about having to get to your biopsy appointment.

On the way out, he'll probably ask about a housewarming party, and if he can leave behind some business cards.

You'll nod numbly
while thinking about the walls with no outlets,

the eight-foot $1500 custom door that you thought was
just a regular old door when you read the plans,

the shower fixtures that are too low,
the cabinets that open the wrong way,
and the beam in the basement
that is sagging.

And that will remind
you that, eventually,
you're going to need
another architect.

And chances are,

Seth Kaufman is the author of *The King of Pain: a novel with stories*. He lives in Brooklyn with his wife and two children.

Laura Lee Pedersen is a Brooklyn-based illustrator who loves cats, comics, and bike racing. She is currently working on a graphic novel.